MEL BAY PRESENTS

Ti...
Tu...

POCKETBOOK DELUXE SERIES
by William Bay

1 2 3 4 5 6 7 8 9 0

© 2005 BY MEL BAY PUBLICATIONS, INC., PACIFIC, MO 63069.
ALL RIGHTS RESERVED. INTERNATIONAL COPYRIGHT SECURED. B.M.I.
MADE AND PRINTED IN U.S.A.

No part of this publication may be reproduced in whole or in part, or stored in a retrieval system, or transmitted in any form or by any means, electronic, mechanical, photocopy, recording, or otherwise, without written permission of the publisher.

Visit us on the Web at www.melbay.com — E-mail us at email@melbay.com

Table of Contents

Fingering Chart	3
Green Grow the Lilacs	4
Tenting Tonight	5
Aloha Oe	6
Lament	7
The Foggy, Foggy Dew	8
The Ash Grove	9
Yellow Rose of Texas	10
Auld Lang Syne	11
Strawberry Roan	12
Johnny Has Gone for a Soldier	14
Ol' Dan Tucker	15
Blow Away the Morning Dew	16
Bell Bottom Trousers	17
Old Shoe Boots & Leggins	18
Wait Til the Sun Shines Nellie	19
At a Georgia Camp Meeting	20
Marchin' to Glory	21
Goin' South	22
Oh, Sinner Man	23
Come & Go with Me to that Land	24
Bile' Dem Cabbage Down	25
Goober Peas	26
Captain Kidd	27
The Fish of the Sea	28
Jolly Old Roger	29
My Bonnie	30
The Bold Fisherman	31
High Barbaree	32
Greenland Fishery	33
Blow, Ye Winds	34
Cripple Creek	35
Sourwood Mountain	36
Big Rock Candy Mountain	37
The Roving Cowboy	38
When Jesus Wept	39
Blessed Quietness	40
There's a River of Life	41
When I Can Read My Title Clear	42
Praise the Savior	43
Great God When I Approach Thy Throne	44
Must Jesus Bear the Cross Alone	45
I am Bound for the Promised Land	46
When Jesus Left His Father's Throne	47
Jesus Calls Us	48
Lonesome Valley	49
The Galway Races	50
Cockles & Mussels	51
The Wild Rover	52
Love is Teasin'	53
The Galway Shawl	54
The Rose of Tralee	55
Brian O'Linn	56
Spancil Hill	57
Si Beag Si Mór	58
Bunclody	59
My Mary of the Curling Hair	60
Musetta's Waltz	61
Drink to Me Only with Thine Eyes	62
Southern Roses	63
Gypsy Dreams	64
Hatikvoh	65
Santa Lucia	66
Do, Lord	67
I Need Thee Every Hour	68
Precious Memories	69
Mandy Lee	70
Daisy Bell	71
Up in a Balloon	72
Strike Up the Band	73
This Little Light of Mine	74
Silver Threads Among the Gold	75
Grandfather's Clock	76
All God's Children Got Shoes	77
Little David Play on Your Harp	78
If You're Happy and You Know It	79
I've Got Peace Like a River	80
Bringing In the Sheaves	81
In the Pines	82
The Battle Cry of Freedom	83
Nine Hundred Miles	84
Down Where the Cotton Blossoms Grow	85
Christ Be Beside Me	86
Our Boys Will Shine Tonight	87
Columbia, the Gem of the Ocean	88
Mama Don't 'Low	90
She'll be Comin' Round the Mountain	91
Loch Lomond	92
Crawdad Song	93
The Mermaid	94
The Old Oaken Bucket	95
Doxology	96

Chromatic Fingering Chart

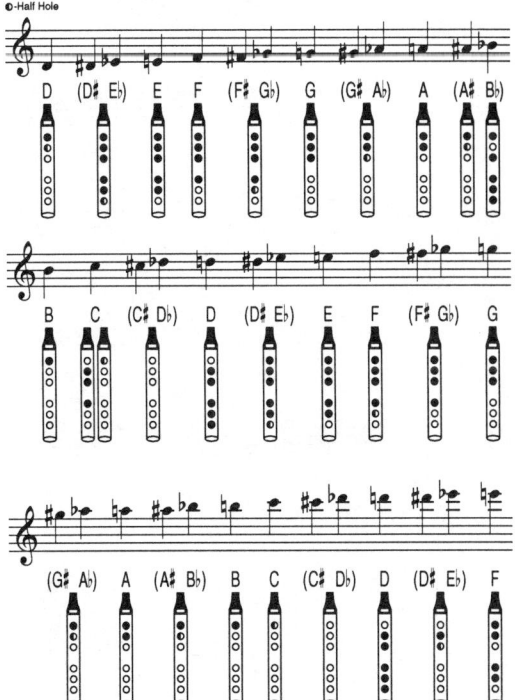

Green Grow the Lilacs

Tenting Tonight

5

Aloha Oe

Lament

The Foggy, Foggy Dew

The Ash Grove

Yellow Rose of Texas

Auld Lang Syne

Strawberry Roan

Johnny Has Gone for a Soldier

Ol' Dan Tucker

15

Blow Away the Morning Dew

Bell Bottom Trousers 17

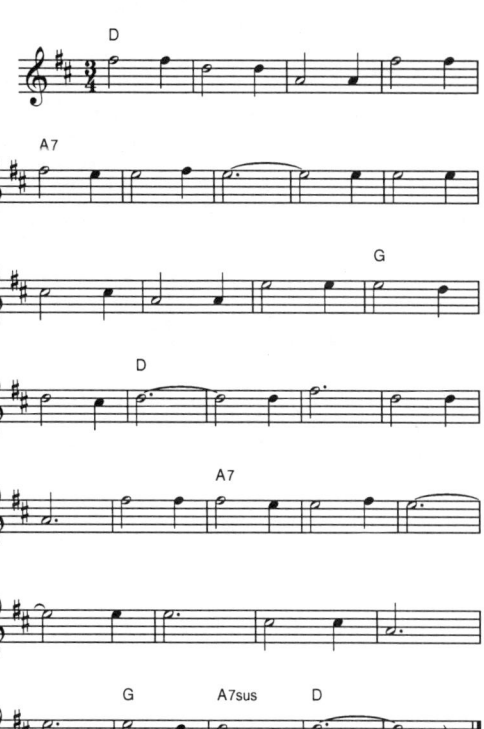

Old Shoe Boots & Leggins

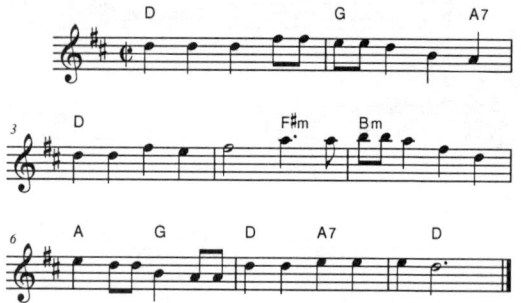

Wait Till the Sun Shines Nellie

At a Georgia Camp Meeting

Marchin' to Glory

Goin' South

Oh, Sinner Man

23

Come & Go with Me to that Land

Bile' Dem Cabbage Down 25

Goober Peas

Captain Kidd 27

The Fish of the Sea

Jolly Old Roger

29

My Bonnie

The Bold Fisherman

High Barbaree

Greenland Fishery 33

Blow, Ye Winds

Cripple Creek 35

Sourwood Mountain

Big Rock Candy Mountain

The Roving Cowboy

When Jesus Wept

Blessed Quietness

There's a River of Life 41

When I Can Read My Title Clear

Early American

Praise the Savior

43

German

Great God When I Approach Thy Throne

Early American

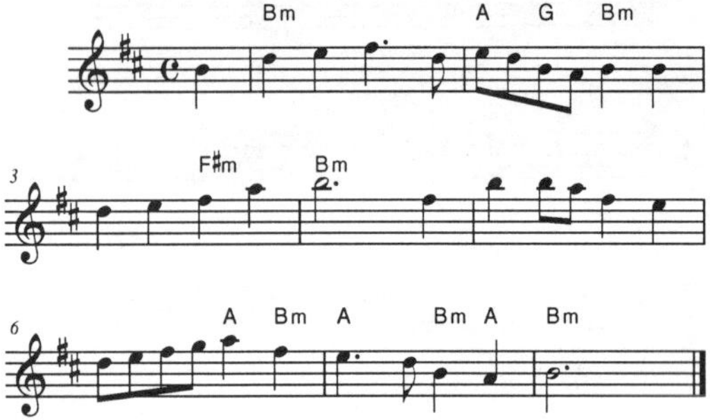

Must Jesus Bear The Cross Alone

45

I am Bound for the Promised Land

When Jesus Left His Father's Throne

47

Jesus Calls Us

Lonesome Valley

The Galway Races

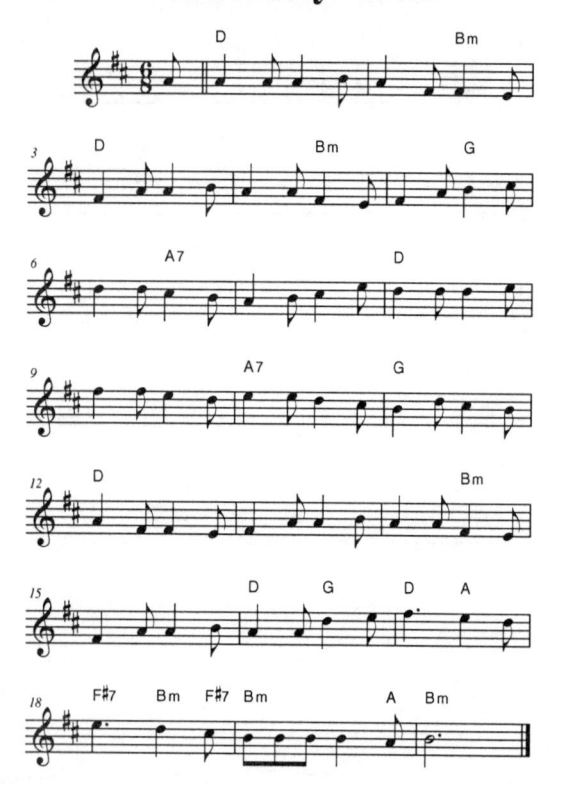

Cockles & Mussels   51

The Wild Rover

Love is Teasin'

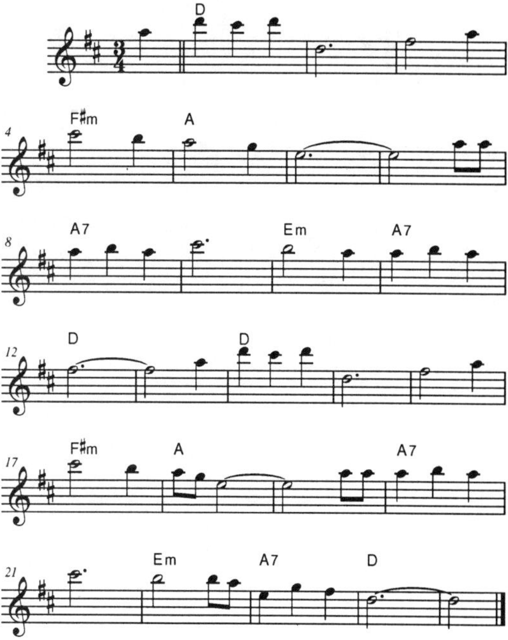

The Galway Shawl

The Rose of Tralee

Brain O'linn

Spancil Hill 57

Si Beag Si Mór

Bunclody

My Mary of the Curling Hair

Musetta's Waltz

Drink to Me Only with Thine Eyes

Southern Roses

Strauss

Gypsy Theme

Hatikvoh

65

Israeli

Santa Lucia

Neopolitan Song

Do, Lord

68 I Need Thee Every Hour

Gospel Song

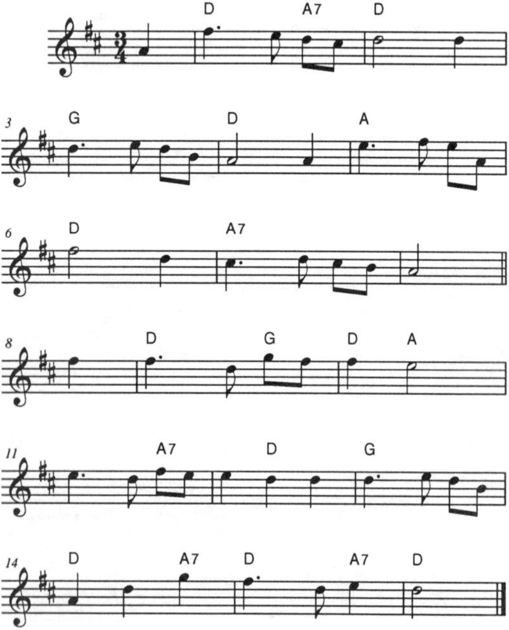

Precious Memories

69

Gospel Song

Mandy Lee

Slowly
American Ballad

Daisy Bell

71

Up in a Balloon

Strike Up the Band

Lively March

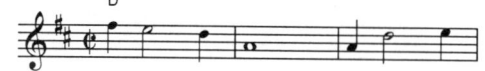

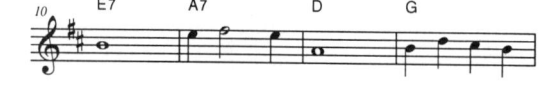

74 This Little Light of Mine

Silver Threads Among the Gold

75

Grandfather's Clock

All God's Children Got Shoes

77

Little David Play on Your Harp

Spiritual

If You're Happy and You Know it

I've Got Peace Like a River

Spiritual

Bringing in the Sheaves

Gospel Song

In the Pines

The Battle Cry of Freedom

83

84 Nine Hundred Miles

Down Where the Cotton Blossoms Grow

Lively Tempo   American Song

Christ Be Beside Me

Our Boys Will Shine Tonight

Columbia, the Gem of the Ocean

89

Mama Don't 'Low

She'll be Comin' Round the Mountain 91

# Loch Lomond

Crawdad Song

The Mermaid

Lively — American Sailing Song

The Old Oaken Bucket

Doxology